WHAT MAKES A COM[MUNITY?]

GROCERY STORES

by J. P. Press

Consultant: Marla Conn, Reading Specialist, Read-Ability

BEARPORT
PUBLISHING

Minneapolis, Minnesota

Teaching Tips

Before Reading

- Look at the cover of the book. Discuss the picture and the title.

- Ask readers to brainstorm a list of what they already know about the grocery store. What can they expect to see in this book?

- Go on a picture walk, looking through the pictures to discuss vocabulary and make predictions about the text.

During Reading

- Read for purpose. Encourage readers to think about the grocery store and its role in the community as they are reading.

- Ask readers to think about the setting of the book. Where does the story take place?

- Ask readers to look for the details of the story. What is happening?

- If readers encounter an unknown word, ask them to look at the sounds in the word. Then, ask them to look at the rest of the page. Are there any clues to help them understand?

After Reading

- Encourage readers to pick a buddy and reread the book together.

- Ask readers to name three things from this book that they could find at a grocery store. Go back and find the pages that tell about these things.

- Ask readers to write and draw a picture about something they learned about the grocery store.

Credits:
Cover and title page, © Konstantin L/Shutterstock and © kurhan/Shutterstock; 3, © hacohob/Shutterstock; 5, © Lopolo/Shutterstock; 5TR, © George Dolgikh/Shutterstock; 7, © ivanastar/iStock; 8, © Dune suru/Shutterstock; 8, © Kwangmoozaa/Shutterstock; 10–11, © Luis Alvarez/Getty Images; 13, © ESB Professional/Shutterstock; 14, © Jeffrey Isaac Greenberg 17+/Alamy Stock Photo; 15, © Bill Oxford/iStock; 17, © Monkey Business Images/Shutterstock; 19, © Hispanolistic/iStock; 20, © FangXiaNuo/iStock; 22, © SeventyFour/Shutterstock; 23BL, © Dune suru/Shutterstock; 23BM, © Ridofranz/iStock; 23BR, © arinahabich/iStock; 23TL, © Drazen_/iStock; 23TR, © LightFieldStudios/iStock.

Library of Congress Cataloging-in-Publication Data

Names: Press, J. P., 1993– author.
Title: Grocery stores / by J.P. Press, Consultant Marla Conn.
Description: Minneapolis, Minnesota : Bearport Publishing Company, [2021] |
  Series: What makes a community? | Includes bibliographical references
  and index.
Identifiers: LCCN 2020029808 (print) | LCCN 2020029809 (ebook) | ISBN
  9781647474454 (library binding) | ISBN 9781647474539 (paperback) | ISBN
  9781647474614 (ebook)
Subjects: LCSH: Supermarkets—Juvenile literature.
Classification: LCC HF5469 .P59 2021 (print) | LCC HF5469 (ebook) | DDC
  381/.456413—dc23
LC record available at https://lccn.loc.gov/2020029808
LC ebook record available at https://lccn.loc.gov/2020029809

For more information, write to Bearport Publishing, 5357 Penn Avenue South, Minneapolis, MN 55419.

Printed in the United States of America.

Contents

Going to the Store

What should we have for lunch?

A **grilled** cheese and tomato soup sounds yummy.

Let's go to the grocery store!

4

This is our grocery store.

It is big.

Where will we find what we need?

FOOD
M A R K E T

11660

SUMMER HOURS
8am-9:30pm
July 5th at Latest Day

ONE DAY DEAL!
Made In-Store
Salmon
Burgers
2 for $5

Back To School
Kids Wellness
Weekend
August 17 & 18
11-2pm

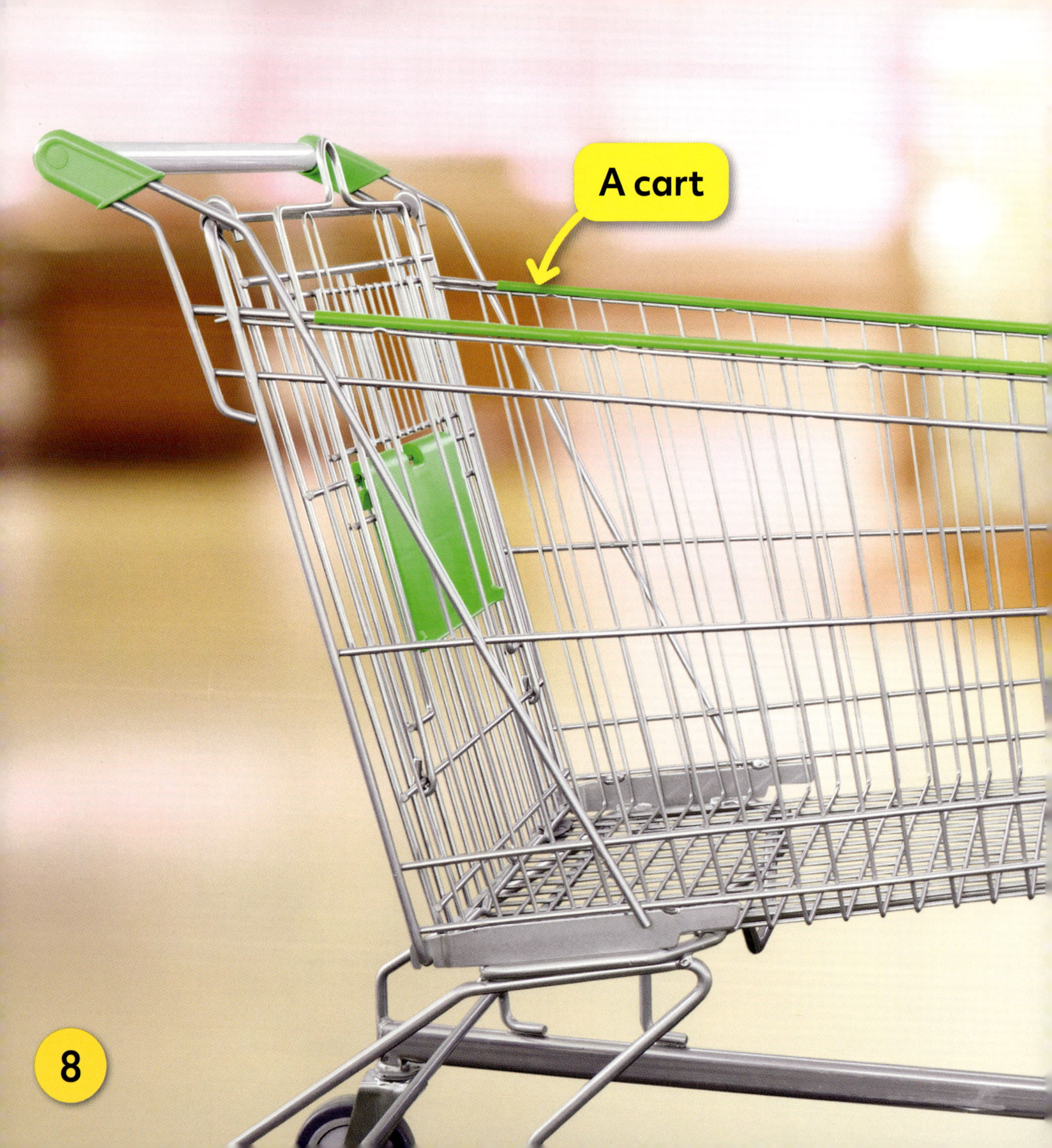
A cart

We get a **cart** when we walk in.

It will hold our food as we shop.

Do you want to help push the cart?

First, we see fruits and vegetables.

Get some tomatoes!

They will go into our soup.

Mmm!

We need bread.

Let's go to the **bakery**.

Put some bread in the cart!

Some places in the store keep food cold.

We go there to get butter.

We pick out some cheese, too.

What else should we get?

We walk down an **aisle**.

There is food on both sides of us.

Say aisle like ILE.

17

We have what we need.

We push our cart to the **checkout**.

A nice man helps us as we pay for our food.